a.m. Dusca

CW01084054

zenspirations
the power of PAWsitive thinking

angie driscoll

published in the UK by Kinloch Publishing

Published in the UK by Kinloch Publishing
A Division of Kinloch Sheepdogs
Copyright © 2011 Kinloch Publishing
www.kinlochdesignandpublishing.com
www.kinlochsheepdogs.com
All Rights Reserved.

ISBN 978-0-9561696-1-7

The publishers would like to gratefully thank the following people for their kind permission to reproduce the photographs in this book.
Agnieszka Filar, Poland
Åsa Eriksson, Denmark
Charles & Nicola Guthrie, USA
Grace Smith, USA
Ikuko Miyata, Japan
Kelvin Broad, Wales
Kerry Driscoll, New Zealand
Kristi Oikawa, Canada
Lesley Mattuchio, USA
Madeline Biancon, Australia
Marta Liberatoscioli, Italy
Michelle Brothers, USA
Rikke Jensen, Denmark

Designed, written and produced by Angie Driscoll.
Printed and bound in the UK by Gomer Press, Llandysul, Wales.

for kelvin

Today you are You,
that is truer than true.
There is no one alive
who is Youer than You

- Dr. Seuss

3

Most things in life are moments of pleasure and a lifetime of embarrassment. Photography is a moment of embarrassment and a life time of pleasure. - Tony Benn

zenspirations

the power of PAWsitive thinking

Acknowledgements   6

Introduction   7

WARNING! Canine zen is addictive   9

Puppy zen   28

On being a top dog   43

About the photos   62

acknowledgements

contributing photographers

A special thanks to the very talented group of photographers who contributed to **zenspirations**. They are all PAWsitively inspiring, generous beyond words, and oh-so capable.
From the bottom of my heart, thank you!

Agnieszka Filar, Poland
Åsa Eriksson, Denmark
Charles & Nicola Guthrie, USA
Grace Smith, USA
Ikuko Miyata, Japan
Kelvin Broad, Wales
Kerry Driscoll, New Zealand
Kristi Oikawa, Canada
Lesley Mattuchio, USA
Madeline Biancon, Australia
Marta Liberatoscioli, Italy
Michelle Brothers, USA
Rikke Jensen, Denmark

editor

My friend, Alec Jasen from Canada, kindly edited this book.
Alec's wife, Bonnie, is the brains behind the book's title.
A rare couple and true friends.

I would like to personally thank all who provided the inspiration and motivation for this book, and contributed ideas and feedback, especially Ann Corbett and Donna Mitchell.

Thanks Kelvin for helping me pull this together. You're the best!

There are moments in life when our resolve is tested, our confidence knocked, we become disheartened, and our motivation ebbs. No matter the sphere of life - friendship, sport, love - we sometimes need gentle reminders of what's most important in life and of the simple truths that change the way we think about the challenges life presents. We often need a pinch of inspiration. *Inspiration is motivation.*

Dogs are a limitless source of inspiration. Robert Caras wrote: *"Dogs are not our whole life, but they make our lives whole."* Very true! The most clever of them all, the border collie, sure knows the secret to living simply, being positive and having an all out rip-roaring good time. Whether they are working stock, playing a dog sport such as agility, frisbee, or flyball, or faithful companions, border collies, with their high energy antics and enthusiasm are a perfect visual metaphor for positive thinking. They truly are canine Zen masters who can teach us so much about life and living.

Zenspirations is a pictorial composition of the everyday border collie juxtaposed with an eclectic, inspirational and often funny collection of quotes and sayings which, together, help keep life in perspective. While many of these quotations apply to life in general, they are also very salient for those who compete in a sport.

In The Oxford Companion to the Mind's discussion of Zen, these phrases jump out to form the perfect, philosophical underpinning of, (if you will) a dog's life:

"Zen is about directly experiencing one's true nature in the present moment. … One is free just to be in the present as it unfolds, carrying no burdens from the past or expectations into the future."

When you observe dogs in action (or in inaction) don't they always seem to be in some form of canine Zen? Aren't they always in the moment and experiencing their true nature?

We truly hope that this light-hearted book of beautiful photographs will give you "PAWS for thought" and much "ZENspiration."

introduction

It is not the mountain we conquer but ourselves.
- Sir Edmund Hillary

Of the many things we can learn from our dogs, living life to the fullest and being PAWsitive may top the list. Even on a bad day, dogs will pep you up, make you laugh and provide comfort and companionship with their PAWsitive behaviour.

WARNING! canine zen is addictive

Why fit in when you were born to stand out?

- Dr. Seuss

In union there is strength.

- Aesop

Jump, and you will find out how to unfold your wings as you fall.
- Ray Bradbury

The world is a looking glass and gives back to every man the reflection of his own face. - William M. Thackeray

15

In a gentle way, you can shake the world.

\- Mahatma Ghandi

You must do the thing you think you cannot do.

- Eleanor Roosevelt

18

There is more to life than increasing its speed.

- Mahatma Ghandi

Patience is also a form of action.

- Auguste Rodin

The path to success is to take massive, determined action.
- Anthony Robbins

The spirit that does not soar is destined to grovel.
- Benjamin Desrali

Unless you try to do something beyond what you have already mastered, you will never grow.

- Ralph Waldo Emerson

25

No act of kindness, however small, is ever wasted.

- Aesop

puppy zen

Puppies are adorable, mischievous, funny, silly, and, in all their youthful innocence, they have a wondrously pure view of the world. Puppies prove that Canine Zen can come in small but potent packages.

What we plant in the soil of contemplation, we shall reap in the harvest of action. - Meister Eckhart

Jump into the middle of things, get your hands dirty, fall flat on your face, and then reach for the stars.

- Joan L. Curcio

Every team goes through their fair share of problems. We're just going to have to play through this. - Rick Carlisle

Gettin' good players is easy.
Gettin' 'em to play together
is the hard part.
- Casey Stengal

33

*There's nothing like biting off more than you can chew,
and then chewing anyway.*

- Mark Burnett

Sweet are the uses of adversity.

- William Shakespeare

When you have a dream you've got to grab it and never let go.
- Carol Burnett

Courage doesn't always roar.
Sometimes courage is the quiet voice
at the end of the day saying,
"I will try again tomorrow."
- Mary Anne Radmacher

You are a child of the universe, no less than the trees and the stars; you have a right to be here.
- Desiderata

39

So be sure when you step.
Step with care
and great tact
and remember that life's
A Great Balancing Act.
Just never forget to be
dexterous and deft.
And never mix up your right
foot with your left.

And will you succeed?
Yes! You will, indeed!
(98 and 3/4 percent
guaranteed).

- Dr. Seuss

We are what we repeatedly do.
Excellence, then, is not an act,
but a habit. - Aristotle

Whether you are striving to make improvements in your life or looking for motivation to improve your performance on a sports field, dogs are an endless source of inspiration. They can inspire a foundation of PAWsitive thinking and focus to many facets of life such as job, sport and self-awareness.

on being a top dog

Game on!

There are no shortcuts.

DESIRE:

The starting point of all achievement.

- Napolean Hill

No life ever grows great until it is focused, dedicated, disciplined.
- Harry Emerson Fosdick

48

The difference between try and triumph is a little umph!
- Marvin Phillips

Success is almost totally dependent upon drive and persistence.
The extra energy required to make another effort
or try another approach is the secret of winning.

- Denis Waitley

Look at me!
Look at me!
Look at me NOW!
It is fun to have fun
But you have to know how.
- Dr. Seuss

Think left and think right and think low and think high.
Oh, the thinks you can think up if only you try!

- Dr. Seuss

Never pretend to be something you are not.

We can do anything we want as long as we stick to it long enough.
- Helen Keller

Creativity: Push smarter, not harder

Genius is nothing more than inflamed enthusiasm.

- Source unknown

There are no speed limits on the
road to excellence.

- David Johnson

61

Book cover	Wishful yearning. Seven week old pup, Steffi. Photo © Angie Driscoll, Wales.
Page 3	Grass is greener on the other side... Photo © Angie Driscoll, Wales.
Page 4	Fools dancing. Photo © Angie Driscoll, Wales.
Page 8	Brynn. Photo © Madeline Biancon, Australia.
Page 10	Five year old Click after winning a big title at an agility competition in Charlotte, Vermont Photo © Grace Smith, USA (http://www.smithfamilyfarmvt.com).
Page 13	Theo and his son, Cap, love nothing more than playing together. Photo © Åsa Eriksson, Sweden. (http://www.busydogs.dk)
Page 14	Play ball! Liam showing his suspension when trying to pluck a ball out of the air. Photo © Åsa Eriksson, Sweden.
Page 15	Eye spy. Bee, a 2-year-old working sheepdog. Photo © Kelvin Broad, Wales
Page 17	A good shake follows a dip in a water trough for Blade. Photo © Kelvin Broad, Wales.
Page 18	Jamie showing off his new trick. Photo © Åsa Eriksson, Sweden.
Page 19	A very bored Lou after a week of wet weather. Photo © Kristi Oikawa, Canada
Page 21/22	Ready, steady, go. Click, Millie, Meg, George, and Remy. Photo © Grace Smith, USA.
Page 24	Kaa is a cheerful, energetic and athletic 4-year-old owned by Lila Logozna, Poland. She participates in dog frisbee, agility and obedience, and loves to run, swim, and play tug-of-war. Photo © Agnieszka Filar (http://www.afilar.yoyo.pl/).
Page 25	When burying her bones in the garden didn't keep her brothers from uncovering her favorite toys, Feather, a 7-month-old border collie pup, owned by Michelle Brothers, USA, came up with a unique solution. Photo © Michelle Brothers, USA.
Page 27	Love. Photo © Madeline Biancon, Australia.
Page 28/29	Playing is thirsty work for Steffi. Photo © Angie Driscoll, Wales.
Page 30	Rose has a nose for Italian truffles. Photo © Marta Liberatoscioli, Italy.
Page 32	Brotherly love. Japanese brothers, Ethan and Koha. Photo © Angie Driscoll, Wales.
Page 33	Dinner party. Photo © Rikke Jensen, Denmark.(http://www.bc-world.dk/)
Page 35	Cash helping with the composting of garden prunings. Photo © Åsa Eriksson, Sweden.
Page 36	Checking to make sure the post holes were dug to the right depth is 5 month old Liam. Photo © Angie Driscoll, Wales.

Page 37   Seven week old Vince, named after Vincent van Gogh. Photo © Grace Smith, USA.

Page 38   Cap likes to sleep under his bed, not on it. Photo © Åsa Eriksson, Sweden.

Page 39   Pixie Treasure. Eight week old Pixie with her leafy treasure. Photo © Angie Driscoll, Wales.

Page 40/41   Balance beam. Cian liked to walk along this old telephone pole, as if pretending to be a gymnast on a balance beam. He was taken by surprise the first time he lost his footing.

Page 42/43   Meg, a talented working sheepdog, likes to do everything to perfection and with great enthusiasm. Photo © Angie Driscoll, Wales.

Page 44   A hot day, a pond, a stick, a human and the game of retrieve is well and truly on. Who tired first? Not Jet or Blade. Photo © Kerry Driscoll, New Zealand.

Page 45   Keeper, owned by Diane Fecteau, Maine, USA, is a very talented agility competitor. Photo © Lesley Mattuchio, Photography By Lesley (www.pbase.com/lesleylou).

Page 47   This one year old, Penny, is a sheepdog-in-training and lives for sheep. Desire is in her heart. Photo © Angie Driscoll, Wales.

Page 48   Jamie. Photo © Angie Driscoll, Wales.

Page 49   Snow is the icing on the cake for 4 year old Roy. Photo © Angie Driscoll, Wales.

Page 50   Ruby, owned by Melanie Clark in the USA, loves and excels in the sport of agility. Photo © C & N Guthrie (http://www.PixnPages.com)

Page 52/53   Sioux chilling out. Photos © Angie Driscoll, Wales.

Page 54   Sweet Holly gazing up to her adoring owner. Photo © Ikuko Miyata, Japan.

Page 55   Little Red Riding Hood's Wolf is 3 year old Rex from British Columbia, Canada. Photo © Kristi Oikawa, Canada

Page 56   Six year old Bailey loves to play football but no-one has told her she is not supposed to eat the ball. Photo © Rikke Jensen, Denmark.

Page 57   Born in the Canadian North perhaps explains 7-year-old Bailey's obsession with snowballs. Photo © Angie Driscoll.

Page 59   The irrespressible Cian. Photo © Angie Driscoll.

Page 60/61   Catch me if you can. Four year old Sioux. Photo © Angie Driscoll.

Page 64   Jamie, the ever-watchful guardian of sheep. Photo © Angie Driscoll.

about the photos

On the road to life there are many paths... some twist, some turn, some dip, some curve. As long as you keep your focus, your destination is obtainable. - Brenda Good